THE LEADERSHIP PUZZLE
Marketplace, Ministry and Life

A Business Leadership Development Course
BOOK ONE

DR. BOB ABRAMSON

Alphabet Resources

THE LEADERSHIP PUZZLE - Marketplace, Ministry and Life
A Business Leadership Development Course - BOOK ONE
Published by Alphabet Resources, Inc.
365 Stonehenge Drive
Phillipsburg, NJ 08865
1-561-963-0778
bnabramson@aol.com

10 digit ISBN Number 0-9843443-2-2
13 digit ISBN Number 978-0-9843443-2-1
Library of Congress Control Number 2010931874

Contact Dr. Abramson by visiting
www.mentoringministry.com

ADDITIONAL COMPONENT TO COMPLIMENT BOOKS ONE AND TWO

JUST A LITTLE BIT MORE
THE HEART OF A MENTOR
Accounts of Cross-cultural Mentoring
and the Lessons they Hold
DR. BOB ABRAMSON
Available at www.mentoringministry.com

CONTENTS

INTRODUCTION

Welcome to THE LEADERSHIP PUZZLE. This is BOOK ONE of a business leadership development course that will guide you through a journey of discovery. It is intended to challenge you to develop a working model for your marketplace, ministry and life. Based on Christian principles and practices, it will influence your decisions in positive, productive ways. It can be used for individual or group study.

The exercises you will encounter are designed to be cumulative in their effect. As you work through them, they will present you with thought-provoking questions designed to cause you to rethink yourself, your life, your profession and your destiny. Be faithful and open-minded to what the processes in this course will have to say to you. Expect to find yourself going deeper into your relationship with God, as you gain new understanding of what He has planned for you. My prayer for you is borrowed from the Apostle Paul. It is simple in its intent, yet incredibly complex. It speaks of the limitless love, favor and sobering responsibility God has placed upon you to prosper, and enrich the lives of the people you touch. Above all, I encourage you to remain teachable and welcome the changes you will discover. Here is my prayer.

(Colossians 1:9-10 NKJV) "For this reason we also, since the day we heard it, do not cease to pray for you, and to ask that you may be filled with the knowledge of His will in all wisdom and spiritual understanding; {10} that you may walk worthy of the Lord, fully pleasing Him, being fruitful in every good work and increasing in the knowledge of God;"

May the Lord richly bless you as you begin this study.
Dr. Bob Abramson

INSTRUCTIONS

01. The WHO I AM Puzzle

You will find a diagram of a jigsaw puzzle on Page 7. It consists of six pieces. The goal of this exercise is for you to look inside yourself and identify up to six key elements that make up who you are. These should be the fundamental building blocks of your identity. Though you may find more than six, pick what seem the six most important. If you find less, label only what you find. You will have opportunity later to add to your puzzle.

Read these instructions carefully. Then, turn to the puzzle on Page 7.

- Meditate on the blank puzzle. When you have thought long enough, begin. Use a pencil or create additional copies to work on. This will allow you to revise what you have written. Please do not convert your responses to ink or final print until a later date. This puzzle process is designed to be revised. It will take a number of sessions and will continue at the same time we are doing other exercises.

- Be careful not to confuse who you are with what you do. This is a common mistake for those who begin the exercise. At this time, we are not looking for a description of how you practice your profession or vocation. (What you "do" will be worked on in the next puzzle.) For example, you may put "lawyer" or "husband," but not "I practice law," or "I support my family." One way to help yourself find answers to each piece of this puzzle is to fill in this statement:
I am a _____.

Remember, we will revisit your WHO I AM Puzzle, as we go through the BOOK ONE mentoring process. Take your time. The answers you find do not have to relate exclusively to what you feel called to accomplish. We are looking for you to begin to discover the complete person. Fill in the puzzle and illustrate for yourself, "WHO I AM." If you will be diligent, your experiences will speak to your heart, and change your life. Be encouraged to use the pages marked "MY JOURNAL OF PERSONAL THOUGHTS" to record as many comments and moments of reflection as possible.

WHO I AM

Fill in the elements (pieces) that make up who you are.
(Your labels will change as the sessions in this study go by.)

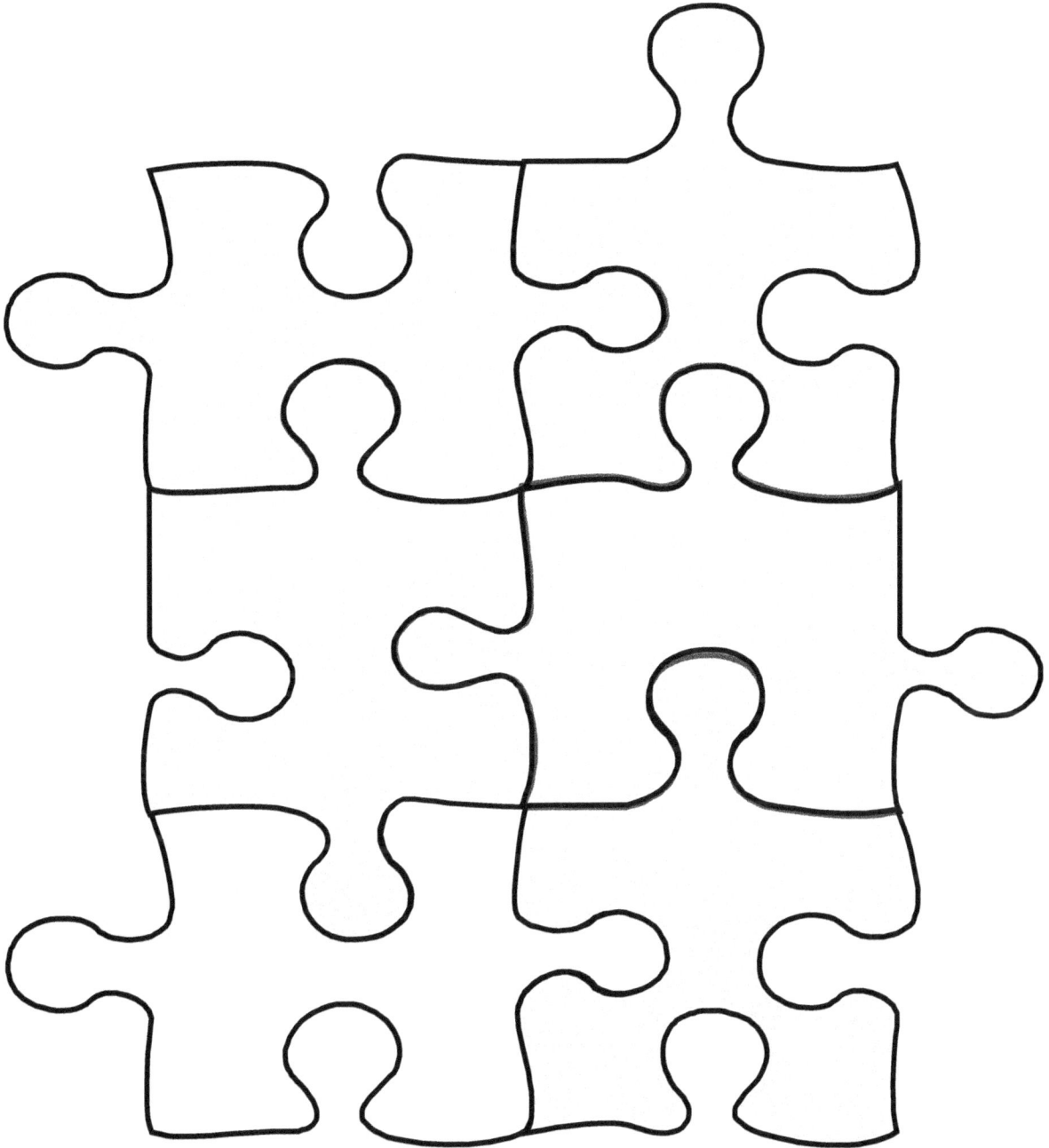

1. Double-check yourself. Eliminate any labels that describe what you do.
2. Discuss your puzzle with your mentor and group.

INSTRUCTIONS

02. The WHAT I DO Puzzle

You will find another diagram of a jigsaw puzzle on Page 11. Like your first puzzle, it consists of six pieces. In your first puzzle, we asked you to look inside yourself. The goal of this exercise is to have you look outside yourself. You are to identify up to six key parts of what you do in your profession, business, vocation, or personal life. (Some or all of these may be your ministry.)

Now turn to Page 11. As before, meditate on the blank puzzle. When you feel you have thought long enough, use a pencil and begin. As with your first puzzle, do not convert your responses to ink until a later date. This puzzle process will also take a number of revisions. It, too, will continue as we are doing other exercises.

Avoid labels describing who you are. They belong with the first puzzle. One way to help find answers to each piece of the puzzle is to fill in this statement:
What I do is _____.

Remember, both puzzles will be revisited as we go through the mentoring process. Here is a helpful hint. <u>Watch for connections that link certain pieces of the two puzzles</u>. They will indicate you are on the right track.

02a. Working with your WHAT I DO Puzzle

After you have filled in your WHAT I DO puzzle, do the exercises on Pages 13-15.

02b. Comparison of the Two Puzzles

Turn to Page 17 for additional instructions. Do the exercises on Pages 19-22. Take your time. The answers you find do not have to relate exclusively to your profession, business, or vocation. There is a lot more to what you do than only these activities. These are exercises in discovering the complete person, to answer the questions, "Who am I?" and "What should I be doing?"

02c. PATTERNS - Go to Page 20 for instructions.

WHAT I DO

Fill in the elements (pieces) that make up what you do.
(Your labels will change as the sessions in this study go by.)

1. Double-check yourself. Eliminate any labels that describe who you are.
2. Discuss your puzzle with your mentor and group.
3. Do the exercises, "Working with your WHAT I DO Puzzle" on Pages 13-15.

02a. Working with your WHAT I DO Puzzle

A. Take the three parts of your WHAT I DO puzzle that have the <u>least importance</u> or smallest relationship to your life, and set them aside for now.

B. List the three <u>remaining puzzle pieces</u> in order of their eternal significance.

(1)

(2)

(3)

List them again in the order in which you enjoy doing them.

(1)

(2)

(3)

List them in the order in which you are <u>most competent</u> at this moment in time.

(1)

(2)

(3)

C. Consider the remaining three parts (the least important) of your WHAT I DO puzzle. Test them and see if they have any relationship with what you have written about on the previous pages. Elaborate on them by connecting them to your personal goals and dreams (if you can). If they have no connection, put them aside for now. Below, write about what you have found. As always, discuss each of these questions with your mentor and group.

D. Do your WHAT I DO puzzle parts fit with each other (relate) without forcing them? If not, you need to rethink some of what you have written and make adjustments. Do so now. Go back and rework your puzzles and worksheets as required, so they make sense.

_____

_____

_____

_____

_____

_____

_____

_____

_____

E. You should have completed Parts A through D. At this point, you now are beginning to form a better idea of where these exercises are going. You may also be experiencing some confusion. It is normal not yet to have things sorted out. Do not be concerned. Keep working. You are doing fine. You will get to a good place of understanding. You still may not have exactly six meaningful pieces in the puzzles. However, what you have will begin to speak to you.

This was a lengthy study. What challenged you the most? Record your answer below.

_____

_____

_____

_____

_____

_____

_____

_____

_____

Are there any new issues or conclusions about which you can write? Do not skip past this page. Share your thoughts with your mentor and group.

02b. Comparison of the Two Puzzles: WHO I AM and WHAT I DO

Carefully review your WHAT I DO puzzle. Compare it with your WHO I AM puzzle and answer the series of questions on Pages 19-21. There should be connections or links between the two puzzles that make sense to you. Identify what does not seem to be working between the two. Continue to rethink and rewrite the labels on your puzzles, especially if you found parts in one that do not relate to the other. Again, this process will continue for a number of sessions, while we are doing other exercises. As always, take your time.

Go to Page 19.

Comparison of the Two Puzzles: WHO I AM and WHAT I DO

A. How do your two puzzles relate to each other?

_____
_____
_____
_____
_____
_____
_____
_____
_____
_____
_____
_____
_____
_____
_____
_____
_____

B. Record one thought from your group discussions that was significant for you.

_____
_____
_____
_____
_____
_____
_____
_____

02c. PATTERNS

Your two Leadership Puzzles have begun to reveal some patterns in your life. Everyone's life consists of many patterns (habitual behaviors). These have been acquired through life's experiences, upbringing, influence of teachers and mentors and any number of other means. These patterns are well set, but every one of them is subject to change. They can be modified and even discontinued. As a person who is in Christ, you have within, the power to do so. You can establish new, God-pleasing patterns.

As you continue through the two Leadership Puzzle workbooks, make it your habit (a new pattern) to identify the habitual behaviors in your life, whether pleasing or not pleasing to God. Begin to judge these patterns. Start with one that is easy to work with, and do the following. If it is not pleasing to God, modify or delete it. If it is pleasing to God, modify or enhance it, so it is working even better. As it becomes habitual in your life, nurture it until it becomes automatic and qualifies as a new pattern.

Repeat this process on a regular basis, one pattern at a time. Keep a record of the progress you make.

LEVEL 1

INSTRUCTIONS

03. THE CALL OF GOD - DOING WHAT IS RIGHT

You are answering the call of God to your marketplace, ministry and life. Your call carries three distinct characteristics. (1) It is an incredible honor. (2) It is a remarkable opportunity. (3) It is an unquestionably sobering responsibility. The call was given when God put something into you before you ever took your first breath. He put it into you so one day He could get it out of you - for His purposes, His glory and His kingdom... all the while, making a way for incredible blessings and prosperity for you.

03a. DOING WHAT IS RIGHT

Email a request to bnabramson@aol.com for a download of the file, "THE CALL OF GOD - DOING WHAT IS RIGHT." It is not on the website. (Permission is granted by Dr. Abramson for copies to be made and distributed to those in your group who have properly procured this workbook.) This is a twelve-page study in three parts. Go through the downloaded study. Reflect on and discuss the questions you find throughout the study with your group. This should take no more than three to five meetings. Then, do the exercise on the Seven Great Rules of Success on Page 25.

03b. EXPLORING YOUR CALL

Do the exercises on Pages 27-29. Discuss them with your mentor and group. Get it done with excellence! If you need clarification or additional guidance, contact Dr. Abramson.

03a. DOING WHAT IS RIGHT

Look at Pages 9-12 of the downloaded study, "THE CALL FROM GOD – DOING WHAT IS RIGHT." Pick out three of the Seven Great Rules of Success that most strongly speak to you. Comment on them as to why they speak so strongly to you.

Rule #

_____

_____

_____

_____

_____

_____

_____

Rule #

_____

_____

_____

_____

_____

_____

_____

_____

Rule #

_____

_____

_____

_____

_____

_____

_____

03b. EXPLORING YOUR CALL

God calls each of us to our destinies. Your call is linked to the truths you find in your WHO I AM and WHAT I DO puzzles. Answer the following:

A. When and how were you called to do what is in your heart? (If you know)

_____

_____

_____

_____

_____

_____

_____

B. What are you called to in the future?

_____

_____

_____

_____

_____

_____

C. Who are you called to, and where will it be? (If you know the answer) If you do not know, to whom and where would you like it to be?

_____

_____

_____

_____

_____

_____

_____

_____

D. What compels you to answer the call?

_____
_____
_____
_____
_____
_____

E. What might keep you from answering the call?

_____
_____
_____
_____
_____
_____
_____

F. What will be the eternal significance of your call for you and for others?

For you

_____
_____
_____
_____

For others

_____
_____
_____
_____
_____

Reflect on what these exercises have revealed to you.

1.

2.

3.

INSTRUCTIONS

04. The Gift of Leadership

In this session, you will answer a number of thought-provoking questions. Be careful to write down answers that have been conscientiously thought out. The gift of leadership is an act of sacred trust by God. We understand this gift is a gift none of us deserves. It is an act of grace that demonstrates His favor. The gift of leadership in the marketplace or your particular profession comes with a call to serve. As with most of the things God asks of us, we have the choice to accept or not.

When you accept God's call to use your gifts to serve, you are agreeing to covenant with Him to care for what is most precious to Him, His people. Never take this lightly. It is a covenant responsibility. It is also a covenant opportunity. Answer the questions on Pages 33-41.

05. God's Champions

On Pages 43-44, you will find a list of qualities that characterize God's champions. It is a list of God's expectations and requirement for leaders. Study the list. Answer the questions that follow on Pages 45-50. Again, take your time. Discuss your answers with your mentor and group.

(Philippians 4:13 NKJV) "I can do all things through Christ who strengthens me."

Go to Page 33 and begin: 04. The Gift of Leadership

04. The Gift of Leadership

Everyone who receives the gift of leadership faces the following issues.

1. What is God saying about your gift to lead?
2. What will you do with what He is saying… and how will you do it?
3. What will it cost you? Are you prepared to pay that price?
4. What will sustain you? What will allow you to get through the hard times and discouragement that will inevitably come?
5. What should you expect as a reward for your willingness to use your gift to lead?
6. Should you have a Plan B?

Let's look at these issues individually and see what we can learn.

1. What is God saying about your gift to lead?

A. How do you know you have heard from God?

B. How clear and how defined was His message?

C. How can you get more definition for using your gift?

2. What will you do with what He is saying, and how will you do it?

A. What is your next step?

_____

_____

_____

_____

_____

B. What do you think the road to your destiny will look like?

_____

_____

_____

_____

_____

C. How will you create a vehicle to get you down the road to your destiny?

_____

_____

_____

_____

_____

D. What will this vehicle look like? How will your gift fit into it?

_____

_____

_____

_____

_____

_____

_____

3. What will it cost you? Are you prepared to pay that price?

    A.   What do you think going down the road to your destiny will cost you?

    B. Where would you draw the line and refuse to pay any additional cost?

    C. What impact, if any, will marriage have on the demands of your journey?

    D. What is reasonable to ask your spouse to put up with, so you can fulfill your journey together? (if married)

4. What will sustain you and allow you to get through the hard times and fight off the discouragement that will inevitably come?

A. How will your faith answer this question?

B. Where is your faith today?

C. What do you think of the following principle? BELIEVE GOD. BEHAVE ACCORDINGLY. TRUST HIM FOR THE OUTCOME. (Relate this to using your gift to lead.)

D. What part of the principle in C, above, challenges you the most?

E. How will you build your faith for tomorrow's inevitable challenges?

5. What reward should you expect for your willingness to use your gift?

6. Should you have a Plan B?

Pick one answer:

Yes. Here is why there should be a Plan B... and here is what it is.

No. Here is why there should be no Plan B.

05. God's Champions

The list below provides a window into understanding how God sees you. It defines your identity as a champion for Jesus. Yes, that is how He sees you. Understand that much of the list may describe potential, and not how you see yourself today. As you read these ten characteristics of God's champions, they will encourage you and help you embrace your call with confidence and zeal. Understanding how God designed you to be, as a leader in His kingdom, is a great motivational tool and a confidence builder. As you go through the list, remind yourself that you have been created to reach your potential in Christ.

(Philippians 4:13 NKJV) "I can do all things through Christ who strengthens me."

GOD'S CHAMPIONS[1]

1. God's champions focus on what they do. Losers focus on what they are going through.

2. God's champions willingly do things that are necessary to create things they love.

3. God's champions pursue completion… but not necessarily perfection.

4. Everyone stumbles. God's champions get up and keep going.
   - ☑ God's champions refuse to accept defeat as long as God is in the battle.
   - ☑ God's champions refuse to set their own timetables. They let God play out the plan. (Acts 27:13-25)
   - ☑ In times of weakness, God's champions pull themselves up in His strength.
   - ☑ In times of personal famine, God's champions feast on His Word and drink of His faithfulness.
   - ☑ In times of sorrow, God's champions turn to His presence and rest in His arms.

5. God's champions know they do not decide their futures. They decide their habits and their habits decide their futures. (Daniel 6:10)
   - ☑ God's champions are well able to look at themselves objectively. They willingly see their flaws and quickly make adjustments.
   - ☑ God's champions are habit-forming people. They are habitual in the Christ-like testimony of their lives.

6. God's champions position themselves for blessings. (Daniel 1:8, 6:10)
   - ☑ God does not send your blessings to you. He sends your blessings to where you are supposed to be, and to where you are doing what you are called to do.

---

[1] Original source unknown - modified by Dr. Abramson

☑ God's champions seek the voice of God, so they will know the will of God... so they can find the blessings of God.

7. God's champions defend their ground.
   ☑ Satan will attack you when you are functioning as a champion. The devil wants to knock you off the high ground.
   ☑ God's champions stand when it is easy to run. They stand when it is easy to surrender. They stand when it is easy to fall. Having done all to stand, they stand!

8. God's champions watch what comes out of their mouths. They speak life and not death. They speak truth, and they speak it in love.
   ☑ They are careful of what they reveal and to whom they reveal it. God's champions never discuss their problems with someone who is incapable of helping them solve them.
   ☑ God's champions submit themselves to people who can cover them spiritually and provide wise answers to serious questions.
   ☑ God's champions speak great things for God. They can only do so because they are wise enough to position themselves to hear great things from God. (Acts 4:18-20)

9. God's champions refuse to just "be." God's champions are "becomers."
   ☑ God's champions understand the value of learning and changing. They engage themselves in the process of becoming all that God has designed them to be.
   ☑ God's champions are disciples first and disciple-makers second.
   ☑ God's champions are teachable. They are excellent students and submit easily to those God provides to help them grow.
   ☑ God's champions are touchable. They live with open hearts toward the Holy Spirit. They also live with open hearts toward those God gives them to love and care for. They do not isolate themselves or allow pride to influence their view of people.

10. God's champions seek out and fulfill their call from the Lord. They do it by living and working with excellence and integrity.

If you were arrested for being a champion for Jesus, would there be enough evidence to convict you?

Do the exercises on the following pages.

EXERCISES FOR GOD'S CHAMPIONS

1. God's champions focus on what they do. Losers focus on what they are going through.

   List four things you can do to increase your focus on what has excellence and eternal value for God's Kingdom. You may also list things that will prevent you from being caught up in busy work, or things that are not God's will for you to do.

   A.

   B.

   C.

   D.

2. God's champions willingly do things that are necessary to create things they love.

   List four of the potentially hardest things you might have to do in obedience to God. Try to define precisely why they would be hard and how you would get them done.

   A.

   B.

   C.

   D.

3. God's champions pursue completion… but not necessarily perfection.

How would you react to people when they do not do something you expect of them?

_____

_____

_____

_____

_____

_____

Consider this principle.

When correcting or disciplining someone you are responsible for, always aim to draw them closer to God. If you can (and only to the extent of your personal responsibility), never let your actions take them farther away from God.

Discuss this principle with your mentor and group.

4. Everyone stumbles. God's champions get up and keep going.

Pastor Dale Gentry has said, *"If you can be denied, you will be denied. You must refuse to be denied."* You will face times when your efforts to do what is right will seem to knock you off your feet. The Bible has much to say about your response in these times. List four Scriptures from which you can take guidance.

A. _____

_____

_____

B. _____

_____

_____

C. _____

_____

_____

D. _____

_____

_____

5. God's champions know they do not decide their futures. They decide their habits and their habits decide their futures. (Daniel 6:10)

This may be your most significant key to success. Your day-to-day lifestyle will affect every aspect of the path you take to your destiny. Think about your current lifestyle, hour-by-hour and day-by-day. What would you change and what would you add to it in an ideal world, to become a stronger, more successful leader? Take your time. Think this through. Answer the following:

What habits would you change or stop doing?

_____

_____

_____

_____

_____

Why?

_____

_____

_____

_____

What habits do you need to add to your life?

_____

_____

_____

_____

_____

Why?

_____

_____

_____

_____

_____

_____

_____

6. God's champions position themselves for blessings. (Daniel 1:8, 6:10)

Complete the following: *Here is how I can position myself to receive my blessings, so I can have good success.*

_____
_____
_____
_____
_____
_____
_____

7. God's champions defend their ground.

Record your favorite Scripture that gives you guidance to defend your ground against disappointment and discouragement. List it in at least five translations. Pick out the translation that speaks best to you and give your reason for it being the one.

A. _____

B. _____

C. _____

D. _____

E. _____

What is your choice for the best translation? Why did you select it?

_____
_____
_____
_____
_____
_____
_____
_____

8. God's champions watch what comes out of their mouths. They speak life and not death. They speak truth, and they speak it in love.

What can you do to enrich the quality of your communication skills? Your answer has more to do with your heart than your speaking techniques. Therefore, look into your heart first. Then look into how you react to what is said to you. Look into how well you listen to others. Now answer the question below. Be sure to discuss your answer with your mentor and your group. Compare answers and ask God to help you to change what needs to change. This process of change is, for the most part, steady and progressive. It will enrich your effectiveness.

What actions can you take to enrich the quality of your communicating?

_____

_____

_____

_____

_____

_____

_____

_____

_____

_____

9. God's champions refuse to just "be." God's champions are "becomers."

Design a concise, six-point outline for mentoring those you lead, or will lead, so they become "more than a conqueror." (Romans 8:37)

A. _____

B. _____

C. _____

D. _____

E. _____

F. _____

Discuss your outline with your mentor and group. Come to agreement on whether all six components are valid. Consider whether the order in which you have written them should be changed. Then, if necessary, adjust your outline.

10. God's champions seek out and fulfill their call from the Lord.

Meditate on Matthew 6:33. What is your understanding of God's kingdom? How will you apply this to your marketplace, ministry and life?

(Matthew 6:33 NKJV) "But seek first the kingdom of God and His righteousness, and all these things shall be added to you."

My understanding of God's kingdom is…

The application of this understanding to my life is…

INSTRUCTIONS

06. First Revision of the Two Beginning Puzzles

Compare your two beginning puzzles once again (Pages 7 and 11). As before, take time to reflect on the pair. Try to reconcile these, and set aside what does not match up. This is a continuing process to get you to focus on what you are sure about in both of them. Again, re-label your puzzle pieces as necessary. We have provided additional copies to work with on Pages 52 and 53. They are side-by-side for you to work more easily with them.

Ask your mentor and group for any input they might have about your two puzzles. (Be aware that their input is limited by their knowledge of you.) Using their feedback, think again about your puzzle pieces. If necessary, pencil in any new or modified labels that now make sense to you. Then answer the questions on Page 55.

07. The WHO I WILL BECOME Puzzle

On Page 57, you will find the WHO I WILL BECOME puzzle. Follow the same procedures you have for the previous puzzles. This is your chance to record your vision of the potential God has put within you. Take yourself beyond who you are today. As always, discuss your puzzle with your mentor and group. Think this through and pray about it. This is an opportunity to hear the inner witness of the Holy Spirit and expand your hopes, dreams and expectations.

WHO I AM

FIRST REVISION

Do your mentor and group believe this puzzle is more accurate than your first attempts? Do you?

WHAT I DO
FIRST REVISION

Do your mentor and group believe this puzzle is more accurate than your first attempts? Do you?

Fill in the following:

The primary characteristics that make up my identity are…

_____

_____

_____

_____

_____

_____

_____

_____

_____

_____

The things I do that are significant to my life's journey are…

_____

_____

_____

_____

_____

_____

_____

_____

_____

_____

There will be another revision of these puzzles before you come to a conclusion about who you are and what you do. Now it is time to introduce a third puzzle.

Go to Page 57.

WHO I WILL BECOME

Fill in the elements to describe who you <u>ideally would like to become.</u>

Do not be intimidated by what anyone else might think. God has bigger dreams for you than you ever imagined. With God, all things are possible. Discuss this puzzle with your mentor and group.

LEVEL 2

INSTRUCTIONS

08. A Pattern for Your Leadership

Go to www.mentoringministry.com. Download the following file: "Free Resources/ Biblical Principles/Paul's Leadership - A Pattern for Us." This study is in three parts. Study it carefully and fill in the exercises on Pages 63-65. Apply these teachings to yourself as they relate to your business or professional life. Discuss the assignment, your writings and answers with your mentor and group.

09. The WHAT I NEED TO DO TO GET THERE Puzzle

This is your fourth puzzle. Turn to Page 67. Meditate on the blank puzzle. Think carefully about the journey ahead. Then, begin. Use a pencil or create additional copies upon which to work. This will allow you to revise what you have written. We do not want you to convert your responses to ink or final print until a later date. As with the others, this puzzle process is designed to be revised. After you have filled in your puzzle, do the exercises on Pages 69-72. (These exercises include a revision of this puzzle.)

10. The IN CHRIST I AM and IN ME HE IS Lists

On Pages 73 and 75, you will find two lists entitled, IN CHRIST I AM and IN ME HE IS. Meditate on them. You will find them to be a collection of powerful, instructive truths. Spend time with your mentor and group discussing them. Pick three statements from each list that touch your heart. On Pages 77-78, write up to fifty words each (no more than fifty) on why you were touched by the statements you picked. You will have six answers in total. This is particularly important. It will help you understand your motives for serving the Lord in the marketplace, and your profession... and especially in your own family. Share your conclusions with your mentor and group.

08. A PATTERN FOR YOUR LEADERSHIP

Exercises for the on-line study, "Paul's Leadership - A Pattern for Us"

A. What would you expect God to say to you, in answer to the "Eight Words that Shape the Destiny of a Leader" (Page 1 of our downloaded study)? In other words, what would the Lord say to the person you have described in your puzzles, if that person asked, *"Lord, what do You want me to do"* with the opportunities ahead of me? (Please, give your own thoughtful answer, additional to the one in the study.)

B. Picture yourself as a *"bondservant."* What does this mean to you? Does it motivate you to serve, even while you are focused on building a successful career? Does it give you some troubling thoughts that might cause you to rethink your approach? Comment please.

C. On Page 8 of the downloaded study, the principle stated is, "Never fall into the trap of trying to demonstrate your own power." When you think about your future successes, what temptations might influence you to demonstrate your own power? (Think about your personality, education, experiences, etc.)

D. On Page 13 of the downloaded study, Dr. Abramson writes about a "walk worthy" of your calling. Fill in the following statement.

My personal definition of a "walk worthy of the call" is…

_____

_____

_____

_____

_____

_____

_____

E. On Page 20 of the downloaded study, Dr. Abramson writes about "Absolute Commitment and Total Reliability… Standard Equipment, Never Optional!" This is perhaps the most important quality you will need. In Dr. Abramson's view, it is on a level with faith. At the bottom of Page 20 of the study, you will see a blank list. Using the space below, complete your list. Use short, concise statements.

List Four Primary Motivational Factors that Drive You
(in order of importance to you)

1. _____

2. _____

3. _____

4. _____

Do your statements agree with your puzzles? Discuss this part of the assignment with your mentor and group. If there is some conflict with your puzzles, it may be you need to pray and rethink some of what you have written (either in the puzzles, or the list, above).

F. On Pages 22 and 23 of the downloaded study, there are "Six Practical Steps to Crucifying "Me, Myself and I."" After spending time in this section of the study, add three more that have personal meaning to you. Use the space provided on the next page.

Practical Step 7

Practical Step 8

Practical Step 9

G. On Page 26 of the downloaded study, you will find a review, listing the "Six Principles of Leadership." Meet with your mentor and group, and discuss what additional principles you might add to the list. Also, see if you would modify the six principles in any way. If so, record your thoughts, below.

WHAT I NEED TO DO TO GET THERE
(TO FULFILL MY PURPOSE AND GAIN MY DESTINY)

Fill in the elements that describe what <u>specific actions and habits</u> you will need to have, to get you to WHO YOU NEED TO BECOME.

Discuss your puzzle with your mentor and group.

Consider the diagram below. Grade yourself on the eternal significance of (1) your current relationships and (2) your current business or professional activities. (1 being lowest and 10 being highest)

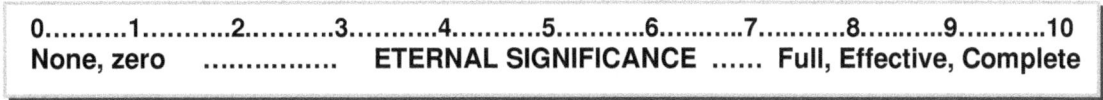

```
0..........1...........2...........3...........4...........5...........6...........7...........8...........9...........10
None, zero    ...............    ETERNAL SIGNIFICANCE  ......  Full, Effective, Complete
```

My current relationships (0-10) _____

My current business or professional activities (0-10) _____

Now return to the WHAT I NEED TO DO TO GET THERE puzzle. Grade each of its pieces using the same chart, above. Then, fill in the grades, below.

Measure each puzzle piece by its eternal significance, 0-10.

Puzzle Piece 1. _____

Puzzle Piece 2. _____

Puzzle Piece 3. _____

Puzzle Piece 4. _____

Puzzle Piece 5. _____

Puzzle Piece 6. _____

Average of the Six Pieces _____ (Add them and divide the sum by six.)

What have you learned from this exercise? Do you need to modify anything in your WHAT I NEED TO DO TO GET THERE puzzle, so you can be more eternally significant? If so, use the fresh puzzle, provided on Page 71. Go there now.

Modified Diagram (Revision)

WHAT I NEED TO DO TO GET THERE

(TO FULFILL MY PURPOSE AND GAIN MY DESTINY)

Fill in any changes you must make because of the exercises on Page 69.

Discuss any changes you made with your mentor and group.

Write a brief summary of why you labeled (or relabeled) each of the six pieces of the
WHAT I NEED TO DO TO GET THERE puzzle.

Piece 1
_____
_____
_____

Piece 2
_____
_____
_____

Piece 3
_____
_____
_____

Piece 4
_____
_____
_____

Piece 5
_____
_____
_____

Piece 6
_____
_____
_____
_____

Discuss what you have written with your mentor and group.

IN CHRIST I AM...

- A child of God *(Romans 8:16)*
- Forgiven *(Colossians 1:13-14)*
- Saved by grace through faith *(Ephesians 2:8)*
- A new creation *(2 Corinthians 5:17)*
- Partaker of His divine nature *(2 Peter 1:3-4)*
- Redeemed from the curse of the Law *(Galatians 3:13)*
- A son (or daughter) of God *(Romans 8:14)*
- Kept in safety wherever I go *(Psalm 91:11)*
- Getting all my needs met by Jesus *(Philippians 4:19)*
- Casting all my cares upon Jesus *(1 Peter 5:7)*
- Strong in the Lord and in the power of His might *(Ephesians 6:10)*
- Doing all things through Christ who strengthens me *(Philippians 4:13)*
- Blessed coming in and going out *(Deuteronomy 28:6)*
- An inheritor of eternal life *(1 John 5:11-12)*
- Blessed with all spiritual blessings *(Ephesians 1:3)*
- Healed by His stripes *(1 Peter 2:24)*
- Exercising my authority over the enemy *(Luke 10:19)*
- More than a conqueror *(Romans 8:37)*
- An overcomer by the blood of the Lamb and the word of my testimony *(Revelation 12:11)*
- Daily overcoming the devil *(1 John 4:4)*
- Not moved by what I see *(2 Corinthians 4:18)*
- Walking by faith and not by sight *(2 Corinthians 5:7)*
- Casting down vain imaginations and bringing every thought into captivity *(2 Corinthians 10:4-5)*
- Being transformed by a renewed mind *(Romans 12:2)*
- An imitator of Jesus *(Ephesians 5:1)*
- A laborer together with God *(1 Corinthians 3:9)*
- The righteousness of God in Christ *(2 Corinthians 5:21)*
- The light of the world *(Matthew 5:14)*

(Source unknown)

IN ME HE IS...

- The Bread of Life *(John 6:35, 40, 51)*
  The thing I will hunger for is more of Your righteousness.

- The Light of the World *(John 8:12)*
  Thank God for Your light, Lord Jesus. I will never walk in darkness.

- The Door of the Sheep *(John 10:7)*
  I am eternally in Your hands, under Your watchful eye, Lord.

- The Good Shepherd *(John 10:11)*
  I shall not want. I need not fear the evils of this world. Lord, Your rod and staff will watch over, comfort and protect me. You never sleep nor slumber. I am safe and secure.

- The Resurrection and the Life *(John 11:25-26)*
  You are my Redeemer. I will spend eternity full of never-ending joy and peace. What an exciting prospect! Thank You Jesus!

- The Way, the Truth and the Life *(John 14:6)*
  Lord, You provide my way, every day. You provide the truth that keeps me free. You provide my daily breath of life. You are the guarantee of my eternity.

- The True Vine *(John 15:5)*
  Jesus, I am eternally joined with You, and will be nourished forever.

- The Great I AM *(John 8:58 & Exodus 3:14)*
  You are absolute in faithfulness... infinite in power... Ruler over all things... *and,* You love me with a love than can never be fully described on this side of heaven. Awesome!

- The Hope of Glory *(Colossians 1:27)*
  All the riches of Your glory are mine. You have given them to me.

- The Faithful Potter *(Jeremiah 18:4-6 & Hebrews 13:21)*
  Jesus, You are working in me to make me complete in every good work.

Review the IN CHRIST I AM, and IN ME HE IS lists. Choose the six statements from them that touched your heart the most, concerning the leadership qualities you will need for the future. Share your conclusions for each statement (fifty words or less) with your mentor and group.

Statement 1: _____

This statement touched my heart because…

_____

_____

_____

_____

_____

_____

Statement 2: _____

This statement touched my heart because…

_____

_____

_____

_____

_____

_____

_____

Statement 3: _____

This statement touched my heart because…

_____

_____

_____

_____

_____

_____

Statement 4: _____

This statement touched my heart because…

_____

_____

_____

_____

_____

_____

Statement 5: _____

This statement touched my heart because…

_____

_____

_____

_____

_____

_____

Statement 6: _____

This statement touched my heart because…

_____

_____

_____

_____

_____

_____

INSTRUCTIONS

11. The Primary Issues of Life

Do the exercises on Pages 81-84. They will challenge you to reflect on your priorities. Share your answers with your mentor and group.

12. Four Puzzles into One: Working Toward A MODEL OF MARKETPLACE, MINISTRY AND LIFE (BOOK TWO)

On Pages 85-88, you will find blank copies of all four puzzle diagrams you have done. Revise and fill them in a final time. See if, and how they have changed from your beginning puzzles.

13. Summary Chart of BOOK ONE

On Page 89, fill in the chart, using your four final puzzles. You will begin BOOK TWO by working from these four puzzles and the chart.

There is an optional exercise on Page 90. It asks you to summarize the entries from your JOURNAL OF PERSONAL THOUGHTS.

Go to Page 81.

12. The Primary Issues of Life

Here are four of the primary issues of life, about which you will have to come to some conclusion. What you decide will define how you move toward your destiny, and the ways you influence others.

1. How will you see people?
2. How will you see yourself?
3. How will you see your assignment from God for marketplace, ministry and life?
4. How will you see God?

Let us look at these one at a time.

1. How will you see people?

The way leaders see the people they lead or work with depends on the following:

A. Social/cultural upbringing (the leader *and...* those who are to be led)

What are the potentially intimidating issues that the social/cultural upbringing of people you encounter may cause you? What about your own roots?

_____

_____

_____

_____

What can you do about this?

_____

_____

_____

B. Your view of the people you observe who presently practice leadership

What are some leadership practices you have seen (the ways a leader conducts himself/herself) that you particularly admire?

_____

_____

_____

_____

What are some practices you believe would be ineffective or wrong for you?

_____

_____

_____

C. Attitudes of a leader's heart

What Scriptures that speak about the heart do you particularly admire and hope to apply with excellence in your attitudes toward others?

_____

_____

_____

_____

Why would any of these Scriptures be particularly challenging for you?

_____

_____

_____

_____

2. How will you see yourself?

Describe yourself in one sentence of no more than twenty words.

_____

_____

_____

- How much of what you wrote is because of how you think others see you?

_____

_____

_____

- How important are others' opinions of you? Why?

_____

_____

_____

In one sentence of no more than twenty words, describe how you think God sees you.

_____

_____

_____

3. How will you see your assignment from God for your life?

Every one of us will be tasked with a primary, divinely given assignment. Though it may contain a great many sub-assignments, the Lord will assign to you one thing that will play big in your heart. In one sentence, describe it.

_____

_____

_____

- How did you identify this assignment?

_____

_____

_____

- How will you stay true to this primary assignment without distractions?

_____

_____

_____

- What kinds of distractions might you encounter?

_____

_____

_____

- What do the Scriptures say about this subject?

_____

_____

_____

4. How do you see God?

How do you see God? This may sound like a simple or even foolish question, but it will determine the quality of your life and affect your level of fruitfulness.

_____

_____

_____

_____

_____

_____

How will the way you see God affect your level of fruitfulness?

_____
_____
_____
_____
_____
_____

If you had to pick one Scripture (or set of Scriptures), above all others, to define what motivates you, what would it be?

_____
_____
_____
_____

Why does this Scripture motivate you so greatly?

_____
_____
_____
_____

Go to the next page.

12. Four Puzzles into One: Working Toward A MODEL OF MARKETPLACE, MINISTRY AND LIFE (BOOK TWO)

WHO I AM
FINAL REVISION

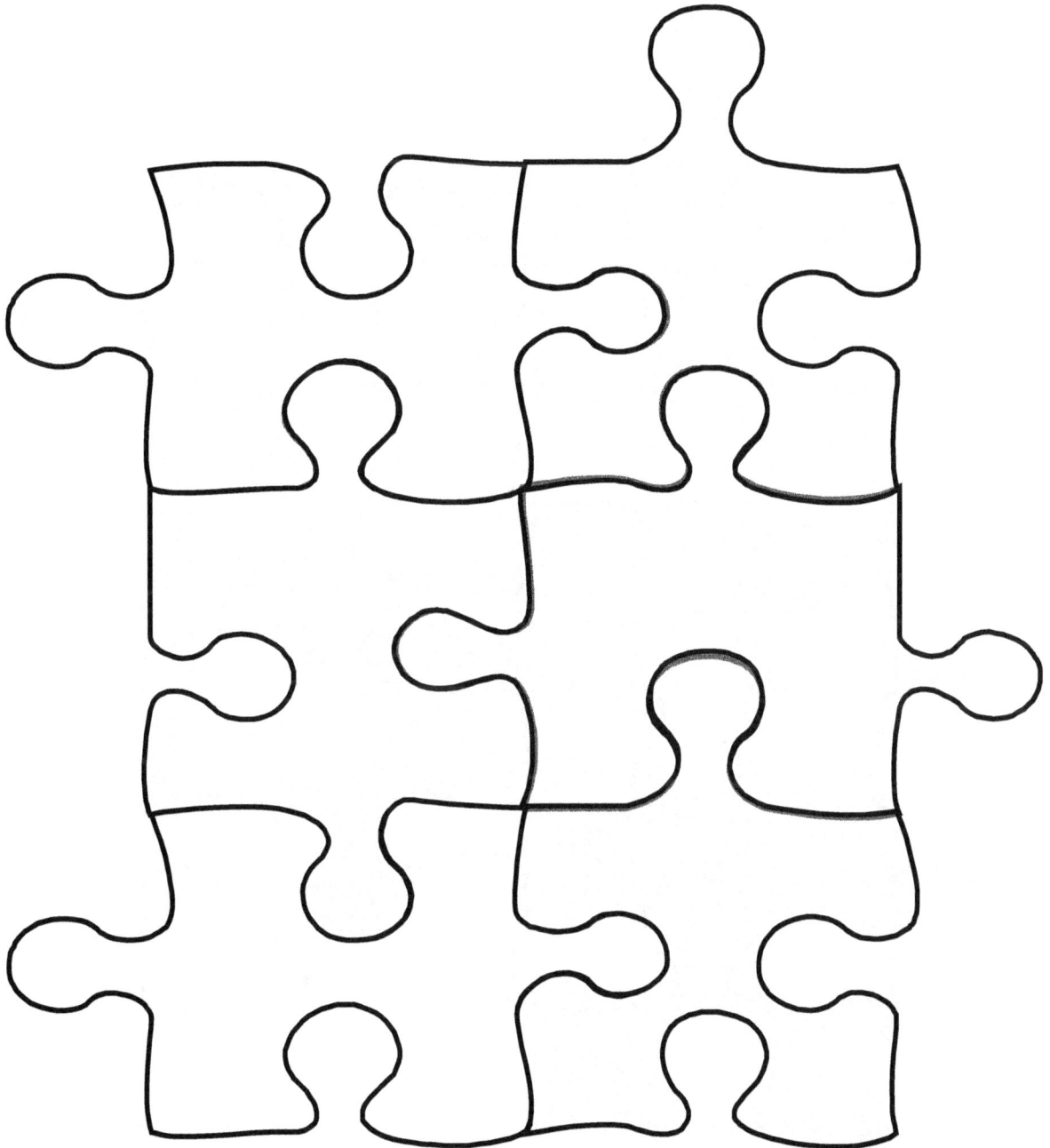

When you begin BOOK TWO, you will work with this, and your other three puzzles as you advance toward your MODEL OF MARKETPLACE, MINISTRY AND LIFE.

WHAT I DO
FINAL REVISION

When you begin BOOK TWO, you will work with this, and your other three puzzles as you advance toward your MODEL OF MARKETPLACE, MINISTRY AND LIFE.

WHO I WILL BECOME
FINAL REVISION

When you begin BOOK TWO, you will work with this, and your other three puzzles as you advance toward your MODEL OF MARKETPLACE, MINISTRY AND LIFE.

WHAT I NEED TO DO TO GET THERE
(TO FULFILL MY PURPOSE AND GAIN MY DESTINY)
FINAL REVISION

Reflect on the exercises from this chapter and on your other three puzzles. Revise this final puzzle.

When you begin BOOK TWO, you will use all four puzzles, as you advance toward your MODEL OF MARKETPLACE, MINISTRY AND LIFE (the goal of BOOK TWO).

13. SUMMARY CHART OF BOOK ONE

Fill in the four columns using each of your four puzzles.

	WHO I AM	WHAT I DO	WHAT I WILL BECOME	WHAT I NEED TO DO TO GET THERE
1				
2				
3				
4				
5				
6				

Your MODEL OF MARKETPLACE, MINISTRY AND LIFE
A Summary of the Four Puzzles

(This will be the focus of THE LEADERSHIP PUZZLE - BOOK TWO.)

If you have been diligent and honest with yourself, you are looking at a good representation, above, of what God has put in your heart, and in a real sense, how He sees you. This chart can be your guide to good decision making about the path you are to walk, on the road to your God-given destiny. An <u>optional</u> final assignment is to write a summary paper describing these four aspects of your call and submit it to your mentor. The paper should be four to five hundred words in length.

Congratulations. You have completed BOOK ONE. You are a winner and a champion for Jesus. I encourage you to go on to BOOK TWO. It has two additional levels (3 and 4). You will find so much more from God awaiting you. As I wrote in the beginning of the workbook, my prayer for you is borrowed from the Apostle Paul. I pray that…

"you may be filled with the knowledge of His will in all wisdom and spiritual understanding; {10} that you may walk worthy of the Lord, fully pleasing Him, being fruitful in every good work and increasing in the knowledge of God;"
(Colossians 1:9-10 NKJV)

With every blessing,
Dr. Bob Abramson
www.mentoringministry.com

OPTIONAL - FINAL PERSONAL EXERCISE
SUMMARY OF MY JOURNAL OF PERSONAL THOUGHTS

Take the best of your previous journal entries (where your thoughts have taken you throughout BOOK ONE) and make a simplified summary of them. Record your summary below. Share it with your group, and others who might be interested.

Dr. Bob Abramson

Dr. Abramson's ministry includes coaching and mentoring pastors, business people, and leaders in the church. Prior to entering the ministry, he was chairman of a sizeable architectural and interior design firm. His extensive business leadership experience provides him with practical insight into the daily issues faced by those in the marketplace.

Dr. Bob Abramson

Dr. Abramson is active in Bible school teaching, leadership training and preaching around the world. He serves as an adjunct professor for New Covenant International University, supervising seminary students in their Masters and Doctoral studies. He has written extensive curriculum materials for ministry training and authored several books. His latest books include, "Just a Little Bit More - The Heart of a Mentor," a textbook and workbook on cross-cultural mentoring; and, "Growing Together," a book on marriage enrichment for every culture.

Over the years, he has pastored multicultural, international churches in New York City and in the South Pacific. He previously established or taught in Bible schools and ministry training centers in New Zealand, Fiji, Taiwan, Hong Kong, Malaysia, Europe and the United States.

Dr. Abramson earned three fully accredited American theological degrees, including a Doctor of Ministry, with a concentration on supra-cultural marriage and family issues. He and his wife Nancy currently reside in Lake Worth, Florida. They have five grown children and five grandchildren.

www.ingramcontent.com/pod-product-compliance
Lightning Source LLC
LaVergne TN
LVHW061227060426
835509LV00012B/1456